Did Y

CAMBRI

A MISCELLANY

Compiled by Julia Skinner

With particular reference to the work of Clive Tully,
Beth Davies and Liz Carter.

THE FRANCIS FRITH COLLECTION

www.francisfrith.com

First published in the United Kingdom in 2010 by The Francis Frith Collection®

This edition published exclusively for Identity Books in 2010 ISBN 978-1-84589-529-7

Text and Design copyright The Francis Frith Collection®
Photographs copyright The Francis Frith Collection® except where indicated.

The Frith® photographs and the Frith® logo are reproduced under licence from
Heritage Photographic Resources Ltd, the owners of the Frith® archive and trademarks.
'The Francis Frith Collection', 'Francis Frith' and 'Frith' are registered trademarks of
Heritage Photographic Resources Ltd.

British Library Cataloguing in Publication Data

Did You Know? Cambridgeshire - A Miscellany
Compiled by Julia Skinner
With particular reference to the work of Clive Tully, Beth Davies and Liz Carter.

The Francis Frith Collection
Frith's Barn, Teffont,
Salisbury, Wiltshire SP3 5QP
Tel: +44 (0) 1722 716 376
Email: info@francisfrith.co.uk
www.francisfrith.com

Printed and bound in Malaysia

Front Cover: **CAMBRIDGE, PETTY CURY 1909** 61469p

The colour-tinting is for illustrative purposes only, and is not intended to be historically accurate

CONTENTS

INTRODUCTION

In the 1950s the area now known as Cambridgeshire comprised four distinct areas: two ancient counties, Huntingdonshire and Cambridgeshire, the Soke of Peterborough, and the Isle of Ely. In 1965 the Soke of Peterborough, an independent authority since 1888, was combined with Huntingdonshire. On 1 April 1974 Huntingdonshire was merged with Cambridgeshire and the Isle of Ely, the new county being known as Cambridgeshire. The city of Peterborough is now in Cambridgeshire, although at one time it was just within the north-east boundary of Northamptonshire.

The geology of Cambridgeshire ranges from sticky gault clays on the uplands to sand and gravel in the river valleys, with limestone outcrops and quarries in the north-west near Peterborough. Chalk and flint with clunch predominate to the south-west. Clunch is a form of chalk that was quarried around Burwell, Reach and Bassingbourne; it was easy to carve, and was particularly used for detailed work in medieval churches. Cambridgeshire and the former county of Huntingdonshire share a similar landscape of rolling hill country; small streams flow into the great river valleys of the Nene, Ouse and Cam, and then through the floodplains that become the wide expanses of Fenland. In the past, the rivers were the great highways between the market towns and river ports of Wisbech, Ely, Cambridge, St Ives, Huntingdon and St Neots.

The greater part of Cambridgeshire is flat – today's Fenland is probably the most fertile arable land in the country, and yet it has not reached this state without considerable effort over the years. The fens were frequently inundated with water until large-scale drainage projects were undertaken in the 17th century, when windpumps were introduced to pump the water from the fen lodes up to the higher levels of the dykes and rivers; later, the windpumps were replaced by large beam-engines powered by steam. The great engine houses (such as the one at Stretham) were fed by hundreds of tons of coal brought by barge along the Old West River. In the 20th century smaller diesel engines made by Perkins of Peterborough were introduced, particularly after the great flood in 1947. Today, the water from the Cambridgeshire basin is controlled by electric pumps, and automatic sluices can be seen at Baites Bite Lock on the Cam, at Houghton Mill and Earith on the Ouse, and elsewhere.

HEMINGFORD ABBOTS, THE CHURCH FROM THE RIVER 1899 44253

CAMBRIDGESHIRE DIALECT WORDS AND PHRASES

'Against' – next to, beside something.

'Backerds' – backwards.

'Bented' – bent or twisted.

'Chuggy' – chewing gum.

'Cut knife' – a hay knife.

'Dockey' – the mid-day snack at work. The most usual interpretation for this is that it gets its name from when wages were 'docked' for the time that workers took off for their meal break. However, the word 'dockey' may actually come from the time when farmers 'docked' their ploughs whilst they took their elevenses.

'Maul' – a mallet.

'Mizzle' – mist.

'No end of' – plenty, lots of something.

'Ockered' – awkward or contrary.

'Pancheon' – a bread bin.

'Scratch' – a bench for dressing slaughtered pigs.

'Slubby' – runny mud.

'Strumpet' – in the former county of Huntingdonshire, now part of Cambridgeshire, this word was used in the past to describe a healthy, hearty child.

'Yelm' – a bundle of straw used for thatching a roof.

'In and out like a dog at a fair' – being busy, hurrying about.

'It fetched the water all out here' – 'it flooded right up to here'.

'It's wetted up outside' – it's rained hard.

'Thin as a yard of pump water' or **'straight as a pound of candles'** – describes someone very tall and thin.

ELLINGTON, THE VILLAGE 1906 55436

HAUNTED CAMBRIDGESHIRE

The Haunted Bookshop in St Edward's Passage in Cambridge (just off King's Parade) is reputed to have a ghost in residence upstairs, hence the name.

The ghost of Dr Butts is said to haunt the room at Corpus Christi College in Cambridge in which he hanged himself in 1632. He became depressed after many students died of plague that year, writing to a friend that he was 'alone, a destitute and forsaken man'. Another of Cambridge's ghost stories may be linked to the plague – a strange 'penguin-like' creature was said to haunt Merton Hall, and has also been seen moving along Newmarket Road in recent years. A local paranormal group suggested it could be the ghost of a 'plague doctor' wearing a cloak and the beak-like mask which in the past was believed to offer some protection against catching the plague.

The ghost of a stonemason working late on Peterborough Cathedral in medieval times who lost his footing in the dark and fell to his death from scaffolding is said to be responsible for a candle sometimes seen burning in a window of the West Front – he hopes it will prevent others falling. Two ghostly monks are said to haunt the cathedral. One walks across the cloisters several times a year, and people who report sightings of him often mistake him for a real person until he disappears through a locked door. The other ghostly monk, sometimes seen inside the cathedral, appears to be very frightened as he walks up the nave looking behind him, and then runs away until he vanishes near the front of the nave. Perhaps a monk was chased and attacked here by Viking raiders, and his ghost disappears on the spot where he was killed.

Ever since the Civil War battle of St Neots in the town's Market Square in 1648, the New Inn on the High Street has been said to be haunted. Some Royalist prisoners were held there after Parliamentarian forces won the skirmish, and sightings have been reported of the cloaked form of a ghostly Cavalier in the building.

The lovelorn spectre of Juliet Tewsley is said to appear near the Ferry Boat Inn at Holywell, near Ely, each year on 17th March, floating from the inn towards the river. Juliet hanged herself from a tree by the river after being jilted by her lover, and was buried on the riverbank. Her gravestone can be seen in the bar of the inn.

CAMBRIDGE, KING'S PARADE 1921 70614

CAMBRIDGESHIRE MISCELLANY

The small black-tarred weatherboarded post mill at Bourn is the oldest of its type in the country (photograph B713009, below). This mill with an open trestle is powered by two common and two spring sails, and turned to the wind manually by a tail pole. Dated 1636, it ceased work in 1925 and is now owned by the Cambridge Preservation Society. It is preserved complete, still in working order, and open to visitors. The largest smock mill in Cambridgeshire is at Willingham, built in 1828. There are two patent sails on the mill, and a very curious fringe of planking to the cap, which may be protecting the gallery which the miller used to service the fantail.

BOURN, THE MILL c1955
B713009

HOUGHTON, THE MILL 1899 44258

Known as the 'corn basket of East Anglia', Cambridgeshire has grown wheat and barley on its rich alluvial soils for centuries. In Roman times corn was transported from Cambridgeshire along the Car Dyke, and in medieval times it was taken by river to the coast and shipped to the Continent, especially from Wisbech. Windmills and corn mills were commonplace in the county until well after the Second World War, and so were the great watermills of the main rivers, like that at Houghton (photograph 44258, above).

A watermill has been recorded at Houghton since AD974, originally owned by the Benedictine monks at nearby Ramsey Abbey. The present brick and timber mill with tarred weatherboard cladding dates back to the 17th century (photograph 44258, above), and replaced an earlier mill that burnt down. The three huge water wheels drove three pairs of grinding stones, and this building continued to grind corn until 1930. Today, the mill is owned and operated by the National Trust and open to the public.

For hundreds of years the Fens existed as wild and desolate marshland of sedge and reeds, with outcrops of land forming 'islands', such as Ely, Thorney and Ramsey. In summer it was possible to graze sheep and cattle, but in winter the rivers overflowed, flooding the peaty countryside so that no agriculture was possible. The Romans tried unsuccessfully to drain the land, but it was not until the 17th century that sufficient technology existed to tackle the reclamation of the Fens. The Earl of Bedford and others employed a Dutch engineer, Cornelius Vermuyden, to drain the land; these men were the so-called 'Adventurers', who 'adventured' capital in return for allotments of reclaimed land. Vermuyden's first attempt was the Old Bedford River, a straight cut from Earith to Denver. This 21-mile stretch bypassed the Great Ouse, and allowed water to drain to the sea more quickly. Vermuyden later improved his original scheme by constructing another drainage cut called the New Bedford River, which ran parallel to the first cut. The strip of land between the two man-made rivers was called the Ouse Washes, as this was allowed to flood during the winter. Sluices at Earith and Denver controlled the flow of water in times of flood, directing it from the mainstream of the New Bedford River into the slightly lower Old Bedford, from which it overflowed into the Washes. Modifications have been made since, but the basic drainage system remains. Other rivers received similar treatment, with straight drainage cuts like Forty Foot, Sixteen Foot and Middle Level Drains duplicating their courses. However, natural drainage alone proved not to be enough to solve the problem. At the same time, water had to be pumped from the fields into the rivers, whose embankments are higher than the surrounding countryside. Windpumps were used in the old days, but modern diesel or electric pumps have now taken over, discharging water into tidal rivers when the tide is going out, then closing the sluices to stop it flooding back in when the tide turns.

The people of the damp Fenlands were very prone to rheumatic complaints in the past. A local folklore belief was that rheumatic complaints could be prevented or alleviated by carrying the forefeet of a mole around in your pocket. Examples of these can be seen in the Cambridge and County Folk Museum on Castle Street in Cambridge.

Although it is 10 miles from the sea on what is now an artificial River Nene, Wisbech has a long tradition as a sea port. Vessels brought in coal from north-east England and timber from the Baltic, and vast quantities of corn also passed through the town's markets. Large granaries were raised along Nene Quay and the west bank of the river from the bridge to West Parade; most of the buildings that survive have now been converted into flats. Even in modern times, boats laden with oranges and bananas would come up to the warehouses on the west bank at the rear of the Old Market, but with the opening of the Freedom Bridge in 1971 this became impossible. The port is not so busy now, mainly through the rise of Sutton Bridge with its better links with South Lincolnshire and Norfolk.

The wealth created by years of shipping has given Wisbech two of the most perfect Georgian streets in England – the North and South Brinks, sombre rows of mansions and warehouses which look out over each other on opposite sides of the river.

Photograph 47591 (below) shows one of Wisbech's now-lost treasures in the Old Market, the Chapel of Ease which was commonly known as the Octagonal Church; this was demolished in 1952, and a branch of Lloyds TSB Bank now occupies the site. In the foreground of the photograph is the drinking fountain, 'for man, horses, dogs and sheep', in its original position – it has since been moved to Lynn Road.

WISBECH, THE OCTAGON CHURCH 1901 47591

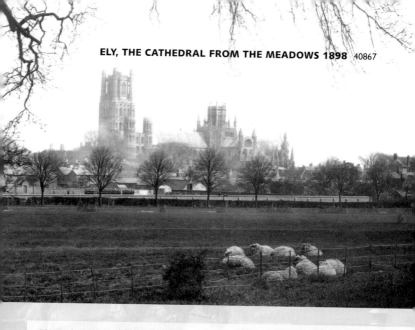

ELY, THE CATHEDRAL FROM THE MEADOWS 1898 40867

Ely Cathedral is one of the most stirring sights in Fenland; it is the fourth longest cathedral in England and has a unique eight-sided central tower. St Etheldreda founded the first religious community here, for women, in AD673, which was destroyed by marauding Danes in AD870; it was later re-founded as a religious house for men, following the rule of St Benedict. St Etheldreda gave a new word to the English language. She was also known as Audrey in the Middle Ages, and a cheap variety of bobbin lace was sold at stalls at the annual St Audrey's Fair at Ely on her feast day. In time all poor quality lace became known as 'St Audrey's', which eventually became shortened to 'tawdry', used to describe something cheap and showy, but of low value.

Eels were once so common in the fenland area that they became a form of currency known as 'booklets' or 'sticks' of eels, with which land rent could be paid to the Church or State. One 'stick' comprised 25 eels. The name of Ely itself means 'the island of eels', and monks at Ely exchanged 4,000 eels a year for the stone to build Ely Cathedral.

Photograph E34010 (above) shows the house in Ely which was occupied by Oliver Cromwell whilst he was governor of the Isle of Ely between 1636 and 1647; it was at one time the vicarage for St Mary's Church, and is now the Ely Tourist Information Centre.

The Anglo-Saxons established a town and a monastery called Medeshamstede at what is now Peterborough, but it was destroyed in Viking raids. St Aethelwold, Bishop of Winchester, came here to restore the monastery and built a large new religious house, enclosing it with strong walls and calling it a burgh; later, the name of the saint to whom the monastery was dedicated was added to the name of the burgh, to create Peter Burgh, which later became Peterborough. When Henry VIII dissolved the monasteries the monastery church at Peterborough became a cathedral, by a special dispensation of the king in 1541; his first wife, Catherine of Aragon, was buried there and he did not want the place to fall into disrepair. The building remains Peterborough's chief glory.

A famous episode in Peterborough's history is the attack on the monastery and town in 1069 by the Anglo-Saxon guerrilla fighter Hereward the Wake ('the watchful'), as part of his resistance to Norman rule. The town was burned to the ground and the church stripped of all its valuables; Hereward used the appointment of an unpopular Norman abbot, Turold, as the excuse for doing this. He took refuge in the Isle of Ely, protected by the surrounding marshes, and held out there for around three years. The Normans made several unsuccessful attempts at besieging the Isle, which included trying to lay a causeway across a narrow stretch of fen, probably at Aldreth or Stuntney. They did break into Ely eventually, but Hereward managed to escape. Legend says that after his death he was buried in the abbey grounds at Crowland, in Lincolnshire.

PETERBOROUGH, MARKET SQUARE AND CATHEDRAL 1904 51544

PETERBOROUGH, WESTGATE 1904 51550

Pits left by clay extraction for the brick-making industry in the Peterborough area are being filled in with pulverised furnace ash from Trent valley power stations, and the surface is then covered with sugar beet washings. This ingenious mixture of waste disposal and land reclamation is returning the former industrial wastelands to agriculture.

Peterborough's trade and population increased rapidly in the 18th century, when improvements to the River Nene made it navigable, and again in the 19th century with the coming of the railway in 1845, which particularly helped to develop its local brick-making industry. The area around Peterborough was an important brick-making centre supporting several companies, some of which eventually developed into the London Brick Company; although this company originated from Peterborough, it derived its name from supplying the capital's increasing needs for building materials.

Peterborough's cathedral rose from the Anglo-Saxon monastery originally founded cAD655, probably by Peada, the first Christian king of Mercia. The core of the present cathedral was the abbey church begun by Abbot Martin between 1118 and 1258. The cathedral has one of the most famous west fronts in England, built in the Early English style (see photograph 69083, below); the dominant feature is the trio of huge arches with their ornate mouldings and pointed gables above. The cathedral is one of only three churches in Europe with a surviving medieval painted wooden ceiling in its nave; Peterborough's dates from c1220, and the paintings include saints and monsters.

PETERBOROUGH, CATHEDRAL, THE WEST FRONT AND BISHOP'S PALACE GATEWAY 1919 69083

Peterborough's magnificent 17th-century Guildhall is supported by columns to provide an open ground floor for the butter and poultry markets which used to be held there (see photograph 51546, below).

The word 'gate' in Peterborough's street names such as Westgate, Cowgate and Cumbergate does not in fact mean a gate but derives from the Danish word 'gata', meaning 'road'. Cumbergate is so-named because it was the area where the woolcombers lived and worked in medieval Peterborough. Woolcombing was part of the process of manufacturing worsted cloth, and was a highly skilled and important trade within the medieval textile industry which was so important to East Anglia in the Middle Ages.

**PETERBOROUGH, THE GUILDHALL AND ST JOHN'S CHURCH
1904** 51546

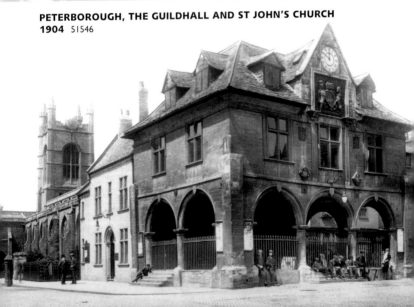

STILTON, THE BELL HOTEL
c1965 S673020

During the Napoleonic wars, French prisoners of war were kept at a prison camp at Norman Cross, near Stilton. They amused themselves by carving models from meat bones and making straw marquetry pictures, and selling them locally. There is a permanent exhibition of some of these carvings and straw pictures at the Peterborough Museum. Some of the models are automated, such as a castle with miniature soldiers, or elaborate guillotines, and are breathtaking in their intricacy. There is also a wonderful model of Peterborough Cathedral.

Stilton is a small village south of Peterborough with a reputation for a cheese which it has actually never produced. The village was an important staging point on the Great North Road, and Leicestershire farmers took their produce to the 17th-century Bell Inn to be transported by coach to London; thus Stilton Cheese was named after its distribution centre, rather than its place of production. Even so, each year there is a cheese-rolling charity race along the village, with local teams, many in fancy dress, bowling a 'cheese' (usually a log cut and painted to resemble a cheese) along the High Street. The winning team receives a crate of beer and a real cheese.

Longthorpe Tower, about 2 miles west of Peterborough, off the A47, is a three-storey building which dates from about 1310, when the tower was added to a manor house. It contains the best-surviving example in northern Europe of English medieval wall paintings, dating from the 14th century, of subjects including the Wheel of Life and the Nativity. The tower is in the care of English Heritage.

Six miles north-west of Peterborough is Helpston, the village where the rustic labourer poet John Clare grew up – photograph H434006, below, shows the cottage where he was born in 1793, the son of a thresher. He was a staunch opponent of the enclosure of the open fields and the destruction, as he saw it, of the countryside and way of life he loved. He published his 'Poems Descriptive of Rural Life' in 1820, and his works have remained popular.

HELPSTON, CLARE'S COTTAGE c1955 H434006

LINTON, OLD COTTAGES c1955 L459041

Photograph L459041 (above) shows thatch and pantile-roofed old cottages at Linton near Cambridge. Cottages like these are timber-framed with clay lump infill. Clay lump was an economical form of material for building houses in parts of Cambridgeshire in the 19th century. The clay, dug out close by and generally leaving a pond in its wake, was mixed with straw to form a thick slurry which was then either moulded in wooden frames into blocks and dried in the sun, or poured straight into shuttering to make the walls. The outside of the house was then rendered to protect it from the weather. It was a tradition in some villages for a young couple who were about to be married to be presented with a number of clay lumps as a start towards building their own home. For those who could afford it, the finished building would then be cased in Cambridgeshire stock brick, or disguised by a plaster render, 'lined out' to look like stone blocks.

Near Peterborough is Flag Fen, a Bronze Age site that was probably used for religious purposes. A large number of poles across the wet fenland, arranged in five very long rows (around 1km), connected Whittlesey Island with the Peterborough area. A small island was formed part way across the structure, which may have been where ritual ceremonies took place. At the visitor centre many of the artefacts that have been found can be seen, including what is believed to be the oldest wheel in Britain, as well as reconstructions of two Bronze Age roundhouses and one from the Iron Age.

CAMBRIDGE, THE CAM, TRINITY BRIDGE 1914 66902a

From ancient times, Cambridge's position on the River Cam, or Granta as it was known originally, made it an ideal trading centre. The earliest recorded reference to a bridge at Cambridge is in the Anglo-Saxon Chronicle for AD875, when the name for the settlement is Grantebrycg. By Norman times the name of the town had become Grentabrige or Cantebrigge, while the river was still called the Granta. Over time the name of the town changed to Cambridge, but the river was still known as the Granta for a considerable period, and indeed is still often referred to as the Granta to this day. The name of the river was eventually changed to the Cam to match the name of the town.

Clare Bridge at Clare College dates from 1640 and is the oldest surviving bridge in Cambridge – all the other contemporary bridges in the town were destroyed by Parliamentarian forces during the Civil War, to make the town more defensible. During the war Oliver Cromwell made Cambridge his headquarters for the Eastern Association. Earlier in his life he had been a student at Sidney Sussex College, and what is believed to be his embalmed/mummified head was buried in the ante-chapel of the College in 1960.

In 1209 a group of scholars came to Cambridge from Oxford, after some of their number had been accused of murder and hanged in Oxford by the townspeople. Many of them returned to Oxford later, but enough remained in Cambridge to form a scholastic community. By the mid 13th century, this gathering of students and teachers was recognised as a University, despite the fact that they had no buildings of their own. In 1284, the first college was built; it was sited next to a church dedicated to St Peter, and was duly named Peterhouse by its founder, Hugh de Balsam, the Bishop of Ely. Over the next 200 years or so, more colleges were added. While monastic properties fell to Henry VIII's Reformation in the 16th century, the colleges of Cambridge remained secure; in fact the king even used the proceeds of dissolved religious establishments to set up his own college, when he merged Michaelhouse and King's Hall into Trinity College.

**CAMBRIDGE, PETTY CURY
1909** 61469

Trinity College's Great Court, shown in photograph 66872a (below) is the largest university quadrangle in Europe. The college has a tradition known as the Great Court Run, which is an attempt to run round the perimeter of Great Court in the 43 seconds that the college clock takes to strike twelve o'clock. It is believed that the only two people to have actually completed the run in the required time are Lord Burghley, who did it in 1927, and Sebastian Coe, who beat Steve Cram in a charity race in October 1988. Technically, Lord Burghley was the second person to have completed the run in time, as someone had done it in the 1890s, but at that date the clock took five seconds longer to complete its toll. Lord Burghley's successful attempt inspired the race scene in the film 'Chariots of Fire', in which the character of Lord Andrew Lindsay is loosely based on Burghley, although in the film the feat is actually achieved by Harold Abrahams. The race scene in 'Chariots of Fire' was not filmed in the Great Court though, but at Eton.

CAMBRIDGE, TRINITY COLLEGE
1914 66872a

CAMBRIDGE, QUEENS' COLLEGE, OLD COURT 1890 26574

Queens' College at Cambridge was one of the first colleges to be built in red brick (photograph 26574, above). The two queens commemorated in the name are Margaret of Anjou, wife and queen of Henry VI, who first founded the college in 1448, and Elizabeth Woodville, wife and queen of Edward IV, who re-founded the college in 1465. The sundial in the Old Court at Queens' College is one of the finest examples of sundial art in the country, but is noteworthy because it is also one of the very few moondials in existence. The shadow cast on the golden Roman numerals tells apparent solar time, and the table of figures below the dial is an aid to telling the time by moonlight, providing the moon is strong enough to cast a reasonable shadow.

CAMBRIDGE, THE BACKS 1890 26495

In the 15th century the Royal College of the Blessed Virgin Mary and St Nicholas of Canterbury, subsequently known as King's College, was founded by Henry VI. The king's first concern was with the establishment of a chapel, and the king's master mason, Reginald of Ely, was appointed as architect. Building started in 1446, but came to a premature halt with the Wars of the Roses; after the death of Henry VI, it fell to Edward IV, and later Henry VII, to continue the building, with Henry VIII overseeing the finishing touches in 1513. The breathtaking Perpendicular splendour of King's College Chapel is shown in photograph 26495, above.

Amongst the treasures of King's College Chapel at Cambridge are the largest and most complete set of ancient windows in the world, and Rubens's masterpiece, 'The Adoration of the Magi', which is displayed behind the altar.

One of the many Cambridge-educated men who sailed to America in the 17th century was John Harvard, a graduate of Emmanuel College. He died in Massachusetts, leaving half his estate to a school which had just been set up in Newetowne, which was renamed Cambridge in commemoration of the place where around 70 of the colony's founders had been educated. The following year the school was named Harvard in his honour, and became Harvard College, one of the most prestigious colleges in the USA.

Many American airmen were stationed around Cambridge during the Second World War. Some of them scorched their names and squadron names with cigarette lighters on the roof of one of the bars in the Eagle pub, just off King's Parade, and these can still be seen. The Cambridge American Cemetery and Memorial is at Madingley, a few miles west of the city. Buried here are 3,812 American service personnel who died during the war, but on the Wall of the Missing, running from the entrance to the chapel, are inscribed the names of 5,126 Americans who also gave their lives in the service of their country, but whose remains were never recovered or identified. Most of those buried or commemorated here died in the Battle of the Atlantic or in the strategic air bombardment of north-west Europe.

CAMBRIDGE, THE MATHEMATICAL BRIDGE c1955 C14080

The curious Mathematical Bridge across the Cam, seen in photograph C14080 (above), is built on geometric principles and was the first bridge in the world to be designed according to a mathematical analysis of the forces within it. The bridge was originally held together – so the story goes – without any fixing devices. Apparently when it was taken apart in 1867 to discover the principles upon which it was built, those who dismantled it could not reassemble it without the use of bolts.

The Church of the Holy Sepulchre in Bridge Street in Cambridge is one of only four round churches remaining in England; it was founded in 1130 by the Knights Templar on the model of the Church of the Holy Sepulchre in Jerusalem. It is usually referred to in Cambridge as the Round Church.

**CAMBRIDGE, THE CHURCH
OF THE HOLY SEPULCHRE
1890** 26524

The Cambridge and County Folk Museum on Castle Street in Cambridge is one of the oldest social history museums in the country. The collection of folklore items is of national significance, many of which were collected by the late Enid Porter, author of 'Cambridgeshire Customs and Folklore', who was a former curator of the museum. Amongst the items of interest in the museum are many objects associated with childhood, ranging from items associated with the rearing of children, such as nursery furniture and clothing, to toys and games. The museum also holds a delightful and important collection of dolls' houses and a good range of dolls.

The last two lines of Rupert Brooke's poem, 'The Old Vicarage, Grantchester', have immortalised the church of this village a few miles from Cambridge:

> *'Stands the church clock at ten to three*
> *And is there honey still for tea?*

It is believed that the clock was actually broken when the poet was living in Grantchester. For years after Brooke's death in the First World War, the clock was kept at ten to three as a memorial to him. The nearby Grantchester Tea Rooms houses an excellent collection of photographs and exhibits about the poet and his contemporaries.

In 1911, James Radley and William Moorhouse formed Portholme Aerodrome Ltd in St John's Street in Huntingdon. The firm made armoured cars, Wight Seaplanes and Sopwith Camels and Pups in the First World War. William Moorhouse was fatally wounded during that war, whilst on a flying mission in 1915, and became the first airman to be awarded the Victoria Cross.

HUNTINGDON, THE OLD BRIDGE 1929 81872

The River Great Ouse through Huntingdon was one of the town's greatest assets as a main route for trading; it remained a significant commercial route until the introduction of the railways in the 19th century, as well as providing the water and power necessary to produce paper in later centuries. The town also benefited from the stage-coaching traffic travelling along the Old North Road, which crosses the Great Ouse over the medieval stone bridge at Huntingdon (seen in photograph 81872, above). The bridge was constructed in 1332 to connect the town with Godmanchester. The respective authorities paid for three arches each, with the builders starting on each bank and meeting in the middle – and working to a different design! The pedestrian refuges built by Godmanchester are three-sided, while those built by Huntingdon are two-sided.

HUNTINGDON, THE OLD GRAMMAR SCHOOL 1929 81880

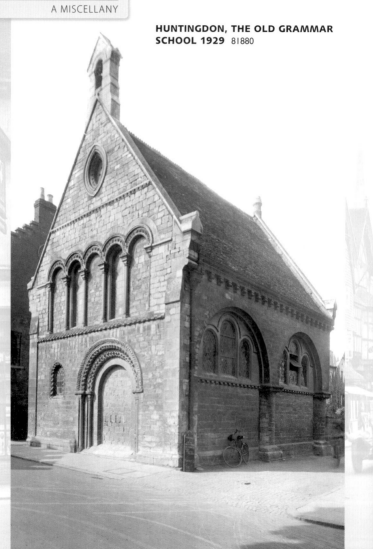

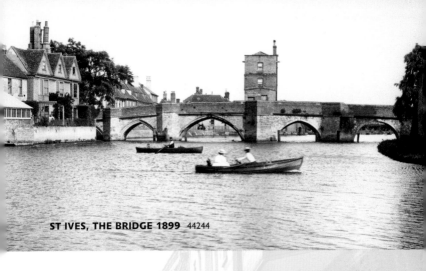

ST IVES, THE BRIDGE 1899 44244

Huntingdon's most famous son, Oliver Cromwell, was born in 1599 in a house in the main street. He was educated at the Grammar School in the town, before becoming MP for Cambridge and ultimately Lord Protector of England, Scotland and Ireland after the Civil War. The 19th-century Cromwell House now stands on the site of 'Old Noll's' birthplace, but the old grammar school in the town which he attended still survives, and is now a museum devoted to Cromwell and the Great Rebellion of 1640-1660 (see photograph 81880, opposite). The museum contains an impressive collection and display of memorabilia relating to the Lord Protector.

The present bridge at St Ives (seen in photograph 44244, above) was constructed in 1414, and the chapel of St Ledger (or St Lawrence, as some records suggest) built on the bridge was consecrated in 1426. In 1645, during the Civil War, one arch of the bridge was removed and replaced with a drawbridge. The drawbridge was demolished and the round-headed arches were rebuilt in 1716. Two extra stories were added to the chapel in 1836 and it became a house, and for a time was used as a pub, but in 1930 the structure was found to be unstable, and the chapel was returned to its original design.

ST IVES, THE CROMWELL STATUE 1901 48069

Photograph 48069 (opposite) shows the statue of Oliver Cromwell which stands in St Ives, erected in 1901. Cromwell had lived at St Ives from 1631 to 1635, and the townsfolk there raised the money for the statue by public subscription. In the political and religious turmoil of the mid 17th century, as King and Parliament fought for power, Cromwell's strong views and forthright manner brought him to the fore very quickly, and through the bitter struggles of the Civil War he was to show himself to be the most able military leader of the Parliamentarian forces. Though he lacked military experience when the war broke out, he moulded a superb cavalry force, provided inspired leadership and rose in three years from the rank of captain to that of lieutenant-general. He was a prime mover in the trial and execution of Charles I, after which he became Lord Protector of the Commonwealth, king in all but name. Ruthless, charismatic and devoutly religious, he was one of the most loved and hated men of his age.

Photograph 84547 (below) shows a now vanished view of the Sheep Market on Market Hill in St Ives – all the sheep pens have now disappeared, and the cobbled section of the Sheep Market has been built over. A paved pedestrian area now covers the pens, and today traders of all kinds sell their goods from stalls at the busy Monday Market.

ST IVES, THE SHEEP MARKET 1931 84547

Photograph H440029 (below) shows the turf maze at Hilton, near St Ives. This beautifully maintained maze commemorates the restoration of Charles II to the throne in 1660, but may have been re-cut from an earlier maze. The Latin words on the memorial read: 'William Sparrow, gentleman, born in the year 1641 aged 88 when he died, fashioned this circle in the year 1660.' One of only eight mazes surviving in Britain, it is of the unicursal type – there are no dead ends, and the narrow grass track leads circuitously to the centre without any deviation.

The village green at Hilton was landscaped by Lancelot 'Capability' Brown, who lived at the nearby Fenstanton Manor. This famous 18th-century landscape gardener was given the nickname of 'Capability' because of his habit of commenting on the 'capabilities' of the sites he was commissioned to work on. His tomb lies in the church at Fenstanton.

HILTON, THE UNICURSAL MAZE c1955 H440029

ST NEOTS, MARKET SQUARE AND HIGH STREET c1955 S37001

The Manor House at Hemingford Grey near St Ives was built c1130, and is said to be the oldest continually inhabited house in Britain. Lucy Maria Wood Boston bought the Manor in 1939 and used it as the inspiration for her series of six children's stories known as the Green Knowe books. The house is open to the public by appointment.

St Neots is named after St Neot, whose bones were brought to the area from Cornwall to give status to the new priory that had been established by Earl Leofric cAD975. In the late 11th century Richard de Clare and his wife, Rohais, had the priory buildings rebuilt on the present Priory Centre site. Nothing of these Norman buildings remains visible today, but excavations have shown they were extensive, covering at least 50 acres. St Neots Priory was closed in 1539 during Henry VIII's dissolution of the monasteries; all its relics, including the bones of St Neot, disappeared, and no one knows what happened to them. The buildings were allowed to decay, and the stone was taken away and re-used elsewhere, possibly some being used on a new town bridge.

39

In July 1648, during the Civil War, Royalist troops were defeated by a Parliamentarian force in a short battle on St Neots Market Square. 12 Royalists were killed and four Parliamentarians. The 'Battle of St Neots' really only rates as a skirmish, but its impact was considerable as the Royalists lost some important leaders in the encounter, including Colonel Dolbier, who was killed, and the Earl of Holland, who was captured.

Bell-founding was an important industry in St Neots for much of the 18th century and early 19th century. The business was begun by Joseph Eayre, who cast a ring of eight of bells for St Neots parish church in 1753. The last of the St Neots bell-founders was Robert Taylor, whose family later established the famous bell-foundry at Loughborough.

ST NEOTS, NEW STREET 1925 77205

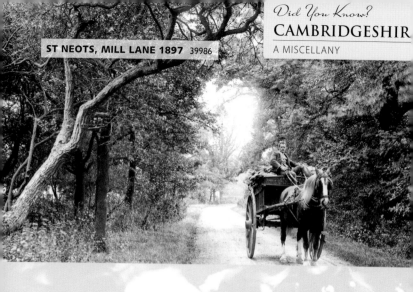

ST NEOTS, MILL LANE 1897 39986

Paper making in St Neots was established in 1804 when the mill at the end of St Neots Common was converted from corn milling to a paper mill by the Fourdrinier brothers. Vast quantities of water are required to manufacture paper, hence the situation of the mill on the Great Ouse was ideal. The advances in paper manufacture made by the innovative Fourdriniers led to St Neots being called 'the cradle of the papermaking industry'.

The making of pillow lace was introduced into the St Neots area in the 16th century, according to legend by Catherine of Aragon, the first wife of Henry VIII, who was confined at Buckden Towers and at Kimbolton Castle following her divorce from the king. Lace-making was being taught in Eaton Socon in 1586, when the overseers paid a woman 2 pence a week to teach poor children 'to worck bone lace'. Later, lace-making became an important cottage industry at both Eaton and Eynesbury.

In the church at Eynesbury, near St Neots, there are some medieval benches. These have ornate carved ends, some in the shape of birds or exotic animals, which are known locally as the 'Eynesbury Zoo'.

The village of Warboys is renowned as the scene of a notorious witch-hunt in Elizabethan times, when ten-year-old Jane Throckmorton, daughter of Robert Throckmorton, Squire of Warboys, accused 80-year-old Alice Samuel of bewitching her; she was experiencing fits, and complained of painful prickling sensations on her skin, like a cat scratching her. The charge was repeated by her four sisters, some household servants, and also by Lady Cromwell, grandmother of Oliver Cromwell, who was visiting the family at the time; Lady Cromwell berated Alice for causing such affliction and forcibly cut off a lock of her hair to burn, in hopes of weakening the witch's power; she subsequently fell ill and died. Alice Samuel, her husband and daughter were arrested and taken to Huntingdon in April 1593, where they were tried for the murder by witchcraft of Lady Cromwell; they were found guilty and hanged on the gibbet at Mill Common. The three purported witches are now commemorated by the image of a witch on her broomstick on top of the weathervane on the Jubilee Clock Tower in the square at Warboys. In recent years a theory has been put forward that the symptoms of 'witchcraft' which the Throckmorton girls experienced (fits, hallucinations and painful skin) might have been caused by ergot poisoning – ergot is a fungus which infects rye grain, and rye was a staple crop in East Anglia at that time.

The name of the town of March comes from the Anglo-Saxon word for frontier or boundary. In past times March stood on the line between Middle Anglia and East Anglia, with trade built up on the fishing or trading based on the Fenland rivers. March is famous for its church – the roof of St Wendreda's Church is a testament to the carpenter's art, a hammerbeam roof with 120 carved wooden angels playing musical instruments. The poet John Betjeman said that it was 'worth cycling 40 miles into a headwind to see'.

MARCH, THE BRIDGE FROM NENE QUAY 1929 81913

SOHAM, HIGH STREET c1955 S597009

The town of Soham owes a debt of gratitude to the heroism of two local men during the Second World War, Ben Gimbert and Jim Nightall. On 2nd June 1944, engine-driver Gimbert noticed that the front wagon of his ammunition train was on fire as the train was passing through the town. He and his fireman, Nightall, detached the wagon and pushed it into a cutting in open country, where the earth banks would smother the explosion. The wagon did explode; Nightall was killed and Gimball badly injured, but the town was saved.

SPORTING CAMBRIDGESHIRE

Cambridge has a long history of rowing, as both a leisure and a sporting activity. Because the River Cam is not wide enough for conventional races, races called 'Bumps' are held. Eights such as the one seen in photograph 61510 (page 47) start off some 1½ lengths behind one another, and each boat has to catch up with the one in front, 'bumping' it.

One of St Ives's famous oarsmen in the 19th century was John Goldie, the son of the vicar. He was three times stroke for Cambridge in the Boat Race boat, and gave his name to the University's second boat.

For many years St Neots has been a centre of rowing, and its oarsmen and women have brought many trophies back to the town. The St Neots Rowing Club's most successful individual oarsman was Laurie Evans, who only narrowly missed Olympic selection in 1928 and who, during his career in single sculls, won 185 trophies.

Born in Cambridge in 1882, Sir John Berry 'Jack' Hobbs, the Surrey and England batsman, was the world's greatest cricket batsman of his time. Between 1905 and 1934 he played in 61 test matches and scored a record 61,237 runs. Perhaps his greatest innings at the Oval was against Australia in 1926, when he made a century to help bring back the Ashes to England. The list of his batting achievements is extensive but here are a few highlights: he scored 197 centuries in first class cricket, the most by any player in any country to date; he is the oldest man in cricketing history to have scored a test match century (at the age of 46); in 1953 he became the first professional cricketer to be knighted; and half his total of centuries were scored after the age of 40. In the year 2000, Wisden selected him as one of the top five players of the 20th century. Hobbs's Pavilion on Parker's Piece in Cambridge (now a restaurant) honours the city's sporting son.

Cambridge United FC hold the distinction of winning the very first League play off final in 1990, to win promotion to Division Three. 1990-91 was also a fine year for the U's. In the FA Cup they beat three Second Division sides, Wolves, Middlesbrough and Sheffield Wednesday before a quarter final defeat at Arsenal, and a fine run of eleven consecutive wins helped the team to promotion to Division Two. The club's best-known player is probably Dion Dublin, who scored the goal that secured the U's promotion in 1990, and was a member of the following season's Division Three title-winning team. He was sold to Manchester United in 1992, and went on to play for England a number of times.

Gary De Roux is thought to be the only Peterborough boxer to have won a British title. He became the British Featherweight Champion in 1991. After retiring in 1993 he became a trainer, his stated ambition being to train Peterborough's next champion.

Rugby in Peterborough has a long history, with matches involving the city team recorded as far back as 1870, when the Peterborough Football Club was formed. The club has produced several players for the England team, including William Yiend, capped 6 times in the 1890s, Michael Berridge, capped in 1949, and Ron Jacobs, who captained England in 1963/64 and was a member of the Triple Crown winning team of 1959/60.

There has been a long tradition of ice skating on the frozen waterways of the Fens in winter, and Mare Fen in Swavesey was held to be the best place in the whole of Fenland for skating in Victorian times – world skating championships were even held there when the conditions were right. The greatest skating race in Fenland history took place in 1895, when the competitors started at Bottisham Locks at Waterbeach, raced to Ely and back, and then back into Ely. Although the distance was 30 miles, the result was a dead heat!

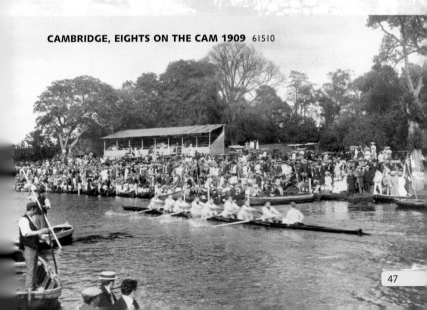

CAMBRIDGE, EIGHTS ON THE CAM 1909 61510

Did You Know?
CAMBRIDGESHIRE
A MISCELLANY

QUIZ QUESTIONS

Answers on page 52.

1. The Oxford-Cambridge Boat Race is rowed over a course of what distance?

2. Which student kept a pet bear with him during his time at Cambridge?

3. One of Wisbech's most notable landmarks is the Clarkson Memorial, designed by Sir George Gilbert Scott – seen in photograph 47583, opposite. Who does it commemorate, and why?

4. What place in history is held by John Bellingham, probably St Neots' most infamous son?

5. What disaster does legend say followed the lighting of an oven in Peterborough in 1116?

6. Why would you have had to pay up in 1895 if you lived in Peterborough and your name was Catherine?

7. What is the link between Cambridge and Big Ben, the nickname for the great bell of the clock at the north-eastern end of the Palace of Westminster in London?

8. How did a Cambridgeshire man come to give us the term 'Hobson's Choice', meaning no real choice at all?

9. Where in Cambridge can you see a Man Loaded with Mischief?

10. What is the connection between Huntingdon's war memorial on Market Hill and Captain Scott, the Antarctic explorer of the early 20th century? (See photograph H136014, page 53.)

WISBECH
THE CLARKSON MEMORIAL 1901
47583

Did You Know?
CAMBRIDGESHIRE
A MISCELLANY

RECIPE

BURNT CAMBRIDGE CREAM

The recipe for Burnt Cambridge Cream is supposed to have originated at Trinity College in the 19th century.

> 600ml/1 pint double cream
> 1 teaspoonful vanilla essence
> 4 egg yolks
> 3 tablespoonfuls sugar

Put the cream and vanilla essence in a saucepan and bring to the boil; meanwhile, in a large mixing bowl beat the egg yolks with 1 tablespoonful of the sugar until they are thick and pale yellow. Remove the cream from the heat and allow to cool slightly, then pour it steadily over the egg yolks, whisking constantly. Transfer the mixture to an ovenproof dish or individual ramekins. Bake at 150°C/300°F/Gas Mark 2 for about 30 minutes, until set. Leave to cool, then refrigerate for several hours.

About two hours before serving, pre-heat the grill to its highest temperature. Sprinkle the remaining sugar thickly and evenly over the surface of the cooked cream. Place the dish or ramekins under the grill, as close to the heat as possible, and allow the sugar to caramelise until a rich brown colour, but watching carefully to make sure that the sugar does not actually burn. Cool, and chill in the refrigerator again before serving so that the topping goes crunchy.

Did You Know?
CAMBRIDGESHIRE
A MISCELLANY

RECIPE

FEN COUNTRY APPLE CAKE

Wisbech is often called 'the Capital of the Fens'. The Wisbech area is known for its soft fruit, but is also famous for its acres of apple orchards, where the Bramley apple in particular is widely grown.

> 750g/1½ lbs cooking apples
> Juice of half a lemon
> 25g/1oz butter or margarine
> 50g/2oz caster sugar
> 2 rounded tablespoonfuls of semolina
> 225g/8oz shortcrust or puff pastry
> 25g/1oz currants
> 3 tablespoonfuls of black treacle

Peel, core and slice the apples. Put the apples, lemon juice and butter into a pan, cover, and simmer slowly until pulpy. Add the sugar and semolina, and bring slowly to the boil. Cook gently for five minutes or until the mixture has thickened. Remove from the heat and leave until completely cold.

Divide the pastry into two pieces. Roll out one portion and use to line an 18-20cm (7-8 inch) heatproof plate. Spread with half the apple filling to within half an inch of the edges. Sprinkle with currants and add the treacle, and then top with the remaining filling. Roll out the rest of the pastry into a 22-24cm (9 inch) round, moisten the edges with water and cover the pie. Press the edges well together to seal, and knock up with the back of a knife. Brush the top with beaten egg or milk and then bake towards the top of the oven at 220°C/425°F/ Gas Mark 7 for 25-30 minutes or until pale gold in colour.

QUIZ ANSWERS

1. 4½ miles.

2. The poet Lord Byron. Whilst he was a student at Cambridge he was annoyed that the university rules banned him from keeping a dog. With characteristic perversity, he installed a tame bear instead, arguing that there was no mention of bears in the statutes. The college authorities had no legal basis to complain, and the bear stayed until Byron graduated, when it went with the poet to his ancestral home at Newstead Abbey.

3. The Clarkson Memorial in Wisbech commemorates the town's most famous son, Thomas Clarkson (1760-1846), a key figure in the fight to abolish the slave trade of the 18th and 19th centuries. He dedicated his life to travelling the country speaking in support of William Wilberforce's anti-slavery movement; in 1996 his efforts were given national recognition when a memorial plaque to him was placed in Westminster Abbey.

4. John Bellingham was born in St Neots in 1776. His job with a Liverpool merchant involved travelling to Russia. When contracts he negotiated there failed, he was jailed. On his return to England he applied for compensation but was refused, which made him very bitter. On 11th May 1812, Bellingham went to the House of Commons and shot and killed the Prime Minster, Spencer Perceval; he was arrested at the scene, tried with some haste and hanged.

5. In 1116 a major fire destroyed the monastery buildings and church at Peterborough. Legend says that the fire was caused when a monk, struggling to light the bake-house oven, cursed it and cried: 'Devil light the fire!'. Work on a new church, the present Peterborough Cathedral, began in 1118.

6. Catherine of Aragon, the divorced first wife of Henry VIII, was buried in Peterborough Cathedral after her death at Kimbolton Castle in 1536. Her tomb was destroyed in 1643. In 1895 a slab of Irish marble to commemorate her was provided and paid for by all the women in Peterborough named Catherine, in honour of the unhappy queen.

7. The clock of Great St Mary's Church, the official University church, chimes a tune which was specially written for it in 1793, and which was later copied for Big Ben in London.

8. Thomas Hobson (1544-1631) ran a livery stable in Cambridge and inspired the phrase 'Hobson's Choice', because he refused to allow customers to choose their own horses – it was his choice, or none at all. He was later Mayor of Cambridge and paid for Hobson's Conduit, which originally stood close to what is now the Guildhall, but was moved to its current site on Lensfield Corner when the Market Square was created.

9. At the Cambridge and County Folk Museum on Castle Street. The 'Man Loaded with Mischief' is on an inn sign, one of four such signs held at the museum which were painted by the local artist Richard Hopkins Leach in the 1840s.

10. 'The Thinking Soldier' war memorial on Market Hill in Huntingdon was designed by the sculptress Lady Kathleen Scott, the widow of Captain Scott, the Antarctic explorer who died in 1912.

HUNTINGDON, ALL SAINTS CHURCH AND WAR MEMORIAL c1955
H136014

FRANCIS FRITH

PIONEER VICTORIAN PHOTOGRAPHER

Francis Frith, founder of the world-famous photographic archive, was a complex and multi-talented man. A devout Quaker and a highly successful Victorian businessman, he was philosophical by nature and pioneering in outlook. By 1855 he had already established a wholesale grocery business in Liverpool, and sold it for the astonishing sum of £200,000, which is the equivalent today of over £15,000,000. Now in his thirties, and captivated by the new science of photography, Frith set out on a series of pioneering journeys up the Nile and to the Near East.

INTRIGUE AND EXPLORATION

He was the first photographer to venture beyond the sixth cataract of the Nile. Africa was still the mysterious 'Dark Continent', and Stanley and Livingstone's historic meeting was a decade into the future. The conditions for picture taking confound belief. He laboured for hours in his wicker dark-room in the sweltering heat of the desert, while the volatile chemicals fizzed dangerously in their trays. Back in London he exhibited his photographs and was 'rapturously cheered' by members of the Royal Society. His reputation as a photographer was made overnight.

VENTURE OF A LIFE-TIME

By the 1870s the railways had threaded their way across the country, and Bank Holidays and half-day Saturdays had been made obligatory by Act of Parliament. All of a sudden the working man and his family were able to enjoy days out, take holidays, and see a little more of the world.

With typical business acumen, Francis Frith foresaw that these new tourists would enjoy having souvenirs to commemorate their days out. For the next thirty years he travelled the country by train and by pony and trap, producing fine photographs of seaside resorts and beauty spots that were keenly bought by millions of Victorians. These prints were painstakingly pasted into family albums and pored over during the dark nights of winter, rekindling precious memories of summer excursions. Frith's studio was soon supplying retail shops all over the country, and by 1890 F Frith & Co had become the greatest specialist photographic publishing company in the world, with over 2,000 sales outlets, and pioneered the picture postcard.

FRANCIS FRITH'S LEGACY

Francis Frith had died in 1898 at his villa in Cannes, his great project still growing. By 1970 the archive he created contained over a third of a million pictures showing 7,000 British towns and villages.

Frith's legacy to us today is of immense significance and value, for the magnificent archive of evocative photographs he created provides a unique record of change in the cities, towns and villages throughout Britain over a century and more. Frith and his fellow studio photographers revisited locations many times down the years to update their views, compiling for us an enthralling and colourful pageant of British life and character.

We are fortunate that Frith was dedicated to recording the minutiae of everyday life. For it is this sheer wealth of visual data, the painstaking chronicle of changes in dress, transport, street layouts, buildings, housing and landscape that captivates us so much today, offering us a powerful link with the past and with the lives of our ancestors.

Computers have now made it possible for Frith's many thousands of images to be accessed almost instantly. The archive offers every one of us an opportunity to examine the places where we and our families have lived and worked down the years. Its images, depicting our shared past, are now bringing pleasure and enlightenment to millions around the world a century and more after his death.

For further information visit: www.francisfrith.com

INTERIOR DECORATION

Frith's photographs can be seen framed and as giant wall murals in thousands of pubs, restaurants, hotels, banks, retail stores and other public buildings throughout Britain. These provide interesting and attractive décor, generating strong local interest and acting as a powerful reminder of gentler days in our increasingly busy and frenetic world.

FRITH PRODUCTS

All Frith photographs are available as prints and posters in a variety of different sizes and styles. In the UK we also offer a range of other gift and stationery products illustrated with Frith photographs, although many of these are not available for delivery outside the UK – see our web site for more information on the products available for delivery in your country.

THE INTERNET

Over 100,000 photographs of Britain can be viewed and purchased on the Frith web site. The web site also includes memories and reminiscences contributed by our customers, who have personal knowledge of localities and of the people and properties depicted in Frith photographs. If you wish to learn more about a specific town or village you may find these reminiscences fascinating to browse. Why not add your own comments if you think they would be of interest to others? See **www.francisfrith.com**

PLEASE HELP US BRING FRITH'S PHOTOGRAPHS TO LIFE

Our authors do their best to recount the history of the places they write about. They give insights into how particular towns and villages developed, they describe the architecture of streets and buildings, and they discuss the lives of famous people who lived there. But however knowledgeable our authors are, the story they tell is necessarily incomplete.

Frith's photographs are so much more than plain historical documents. They are living proofs of the flow of human life down the generations. They show real people at real moments in history; and each of those people is the son or daughter of someone, the brother or sister, aunt or uncle, grandfather or grandmother of someone else. All of them lived, worked and played in the streets depicted in Frith's photographs.

We would be grateful if you would give us your insights into the places shown in our photographs: the streets and buildings, the shops, businesses and industries. Post your memories of life in those streets on the Frith website: what it was like growing up there, who ran the local shop and what shopping was like years ago; if your workplace is shown tell us about your working day and what the building is used for now. Read other visitors' memories and reconnect with your shared local history and heritage. With your help more and more Frith photographs can be brought to life, and vital memories preserved for posterity, and for the benefit of historians in the future.

Wherever possible, we will try to include some of your comments in future editions of our books. Moreover, if you spot errors in dates, titles or other facts, please let us know, because our archive records are not always completely accurate—they rely on 140 years of human endeavour and hand-compiled records. You can email us using the contact form on the website.

Thank you!

For further information, trade, or author enquiries
please contact us at the address below:

The Francis Frith Collection, Frith's Barn, Teffont, Salisbury, Wiltshire, England SP3 5QP.

Tel: +44 (0)1722 716 376 Fax: +44 (0)1722 716 881
e-mail: sales@francisfrith.co.uk **www.francisfrith.com**